The Life of
Rosa Parks

Cynthia Mercati

Contents

Rigby
A Harcourt Achieve Imprint

www.Rigby.com
1-800-531-5015

Growing Up in Alabama

Rosa Parks was born in 1913 in Alabama. At that time there were **segregation** laws in the South. These unfair laws did not allow African Americans and Caucasians, or white people, to live in the same places, go to the same schools, or use the same bathrooms or water fountains.

different water fountains for African Americans

Even as a child, Rosa felt that people should not treat others unfairly. This is something she believed in her whole life.

Going to School

After Rosa finished the 6th grade in 1924, she and her mother moved to Montgomery, Alabama, so she could finish school there. When Rosa was in 11th grade, her grandmother became very sick. Rosa had to leave school and take care of her.

different schools for African American children

young women
working in a factory

After her grandmother died, Rosa started working in a factory. Soon she met Raymond Parks, and they got married in 1932. The next year Rosa finished high school.

Riding the Bus

In Montgomery there were laws about bus segregation. The front part of the bus was for Caucasian people, so African Americans had to sit in the back of the bus. African Americans could never sit in the front of the bus. If the bus was full, and more Caucasian passengers got on, the driver could ask the African Americans to give their seats to the Caucasian passengers. These laws made African Americans very angry.

African Americans riding at the back of the bus

One day in 1943, a bus driver
told Rosa to get off the bus so that
a Caucasian person could have
her seat. He grabbed her coat and
yelled, "Get off my bus!"

Rosa got off the bus. She became very angry, and she knew that one day she would try to change the unfair bus laws.

Rosa Joins the NAACP

Rosa joined the National Association for the Advancement of Colored People, or the NAACP. The NAACP is a group that helps African Americans fight against unfair laws. Through the NAACP Rosa learned that **discrimination** happens when some people treat others differently for unfair reasons.

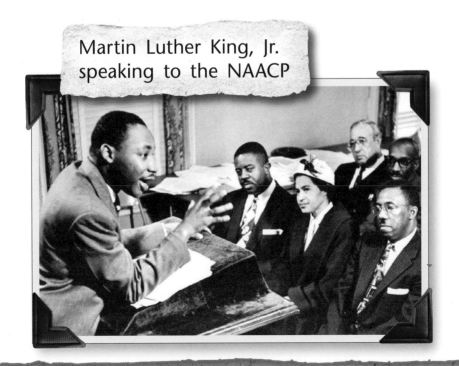

Martin Luther King, Jr. speaking to the NAACP

Rosa Goes to Jail

On December 1, 1955, Rosa got on a bus and took a seat in the back. Soon all of the seats were filled, but there was still one Caucasian man who was standing.

The bus driver told some of the African Americans to stand up, but Rosa didn't.

Rosa at the jail

The bus driver asked Rosa, "Are you going to stand up?"

"No," Rosa replied.

The driver told her that he was going to call the police. Rosa knew that she could either stand up or go to jail. Rosa made up her mind and went to jail.

The Bus Boycott

After the NAACP paid for Rosa to get out of jail, they had a meeting. They wanted every African American in Montgomery to **boycott** the buses. Every African American would stop riding the bus to work, home, or to school.

On Monday morning thousands of African Americans walked to work instead of riding the buses. In fact, they didn't ride the buses for 381 days.

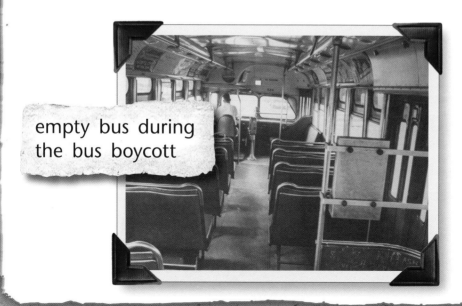

empty bus during the bus boycott

Finally on December 20, 1956, the **Supreme Court,** which is the highest court in the United States, ruled that segregation on Montgomery buses was **illegal.** The next morning African Americans got back on the buses and sat anywhere they wanted to sit.

The African American **citizens** of Montgomery had won their fight against bus segregation. Rosa Parks had helped to make the world a better place.

Rosa on December 21, 1956, in the front of the bus

Time Line

1932
Rosa gets married.

1913
Rosa Parks is born in Tuskegee, Alabama.

1943
Rosa joins the NAACP.

1910 1920 1930 1940 1950

1924
Rosa moves to Montgomery, Alabama.

1933
Rosa finishes high school.

1956

The Montgomery bus boycott ends. The Supreme Court decides that segregation on Montgomery buses is illegal.

| 1960 | 1970 | 1980 | 1990 | 2000 |

1955

The African American citizens of Montgomery, Alabama, boycott the buses.

2005

Rosa Parks dies.

Glossary

boycott to refuse to buy or use something

citizen a person who lives in a city, state, or country

discrimination when people treat others differently for unfair reasons

illegal against the law

segregation the separation of a person or a group of people from others

Supreme Court the highest court in the United States